PLAYING WITH
paint

Sara Lynn & Diane James

Cartwheel
·B·O·O·K·S·™

Scholastic Inc
New York Toronto London Auckland Sydney

➋ Patterns

Since painting can be messy, always wear a smock and spread newspaper down before you paint.

To make a simple printed pattern, crumple a piece of paper. Dip the paper into a dish of paint. Press it onto a sheet of colored paper.

Cut a piece from a sponge. Mix some thick paint in a dish and dip the sponge in the paint. Make a print on a sheet of colored paper. Try making another print without adding any more paint. Is it as clear as the first one? Try painting a picture with a sponge.

To make a swirly straw painting, mix some runny paint and drip a little onto a sheet of paper. Put the end of a straw close to the paint and blow hard! Try using a different color while the first one is wet.

Splattering is another messy way of painting, so always put lots of newspaper down first. Dip a thick paintbrush in water base paint. Flick the paintbrush over a sheet of paper and watch out for the splatters of paint. Now have fun with our other ideas!

4 Fun Prints

You can make prints by putting finger paint onto an object and pressing the object down on a piece of paper. Try putting some paint on your finger and pressing it on your paper. We used toy building blocks, a balloon, a fork, and a glue spreader. Can you think of other ideas?

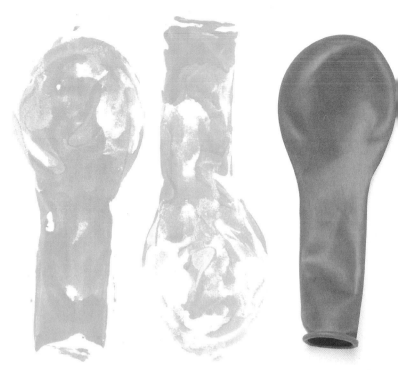

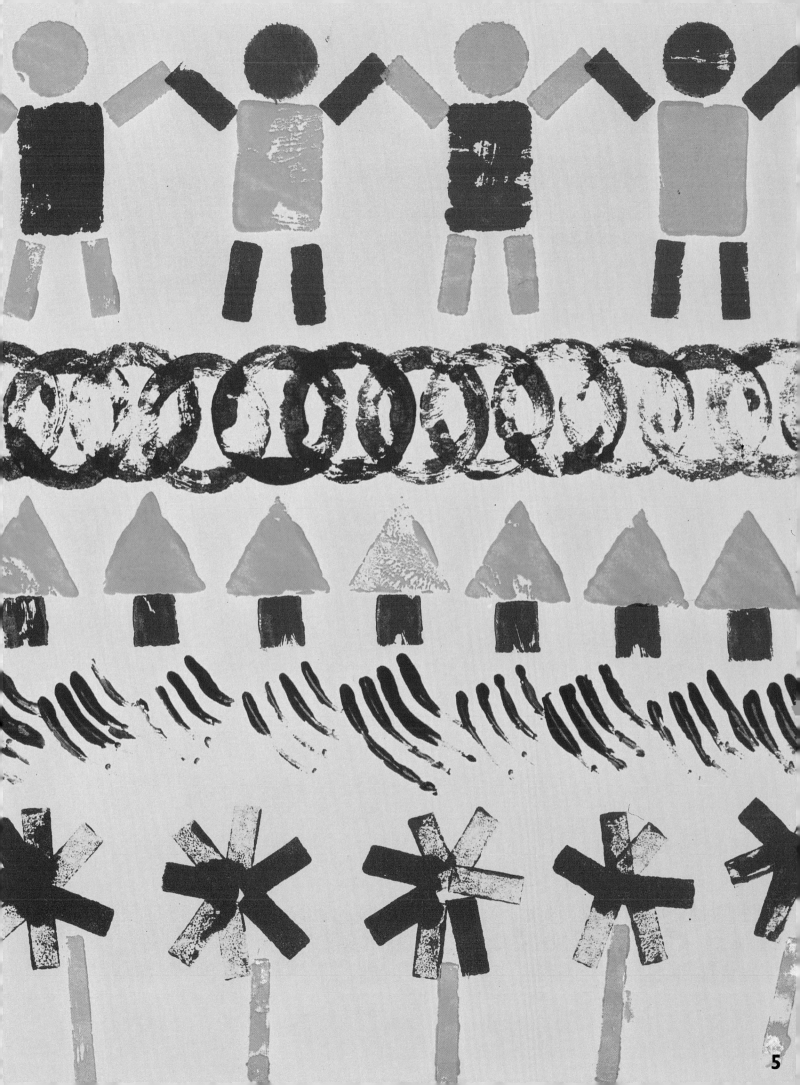

❻ Painted Eggs

Ask a grown-up to hard boil some eggs for you. Then let them cool. Use nontoxic poster paint to paint all over the egg. It may help to prop the egg up in an egg carton. When the paint is dry, put the egg on newspaper. Now turn the page to find out how we made these painted eggs.

Ask a grown-up to hard boil some eggs for you. Then let them cool. Paint the eggs all over in bright colors. Let them dry.

Now you are ready to decorate your eggs. Think carefully about the colors you are going to use. Put lots of newspaper on the floor or table. Some of these methods are messy!

We used a paintbrush with stiff bristles to paint the egg below.
For this method it is best to use a thick tempera paint. Make short brush strokes over one side of the egg – don't forget the top and bottom! When the paint is dry, turn the egg over and paint the other side the same way.

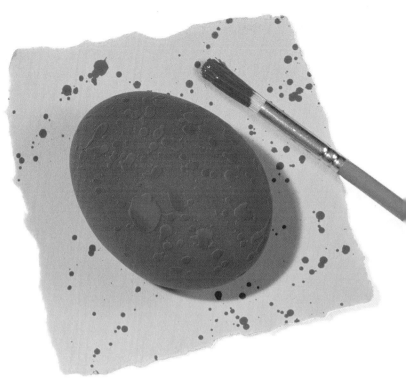

We had a lot of fun splattering paint over the egg above but it sure was messy! Put an egg on a large sheet of newspaper. Dip a paintbrush in some thin water-base paint and flick it over the egg. Splatter one side and allow it to dry before you turn the egg over to do the other side.

To decorate the egg on the right, we used a piece of crumpled paper instead of a paintbrush. Scrunch up a small piece of newspaper and dip it in some thick paint. Dab the paper onto an egg. You will need more paint after a few dabs.

⑩ Potato Prints

Here is an easy way to make your own wrapping paper.

First draw a shape on one half of a potato. Ask a grown-up to cut out the shapes as we've done here.

Pour your paint into a dish. Dip your potato into the paint. Press the potato firmly on the paper. Dip the potato into the paint. Keep printing until the paper is covered.

You can use potato prints on fabric as well as paper! To make sure that your prints do not wash out, you will need to use special fabric paints, which you can buy at a hobby shop. Keep your shapes as simple as possible. To make the happy people here, we printed green triangles on the fabric. When these were dry, we painted on the heads, arms, and legs with a paintbrush.

⑭ Macaroni Beads

These beads look good enough to eat! They are made from dry macaroni. To make a necklace, choose macaroni with a hole through the middle. Paint the macaroni with fairly thick paint. Thread the pieces onto thick cord or a shoelace.

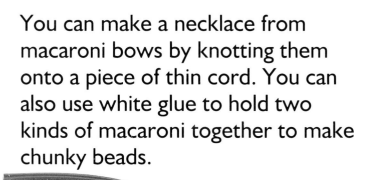

You can make a necklace from macaroni bows by knotting them onto a piece of thin cord. You can also use white glue to hold two kinds of macaroni together to make chunky beads.

⓰ Stencils

All of the patterns and letters here were made by using stencils. You can find out how to make them on page 18. Stencils are good for covering large areas quickly.

You could use your stencils to decorate notebooks or poster paper. Can you think of other ways to use stencils?

You can buy stencils at a store, but you can make your own using thick cardboard. Draw a simple shape on a piece of cardboard. Ask a grown-up to cut your shape out. The piece of cardboard is now your stencil. Hold the stencil down firmly with one hand. With the other hand, use a sponge dipped in paint to dab over the shape.

When you lift the stencil off, you will see your shape! You can use your stencil over and over again. Make a collection and try using different stencils to make a pattern.

⑳ Block Prints

Here is another quick way to decorate paper. You can make your own wrapping paper, or you can use your printed paper to make a cover for a notebook. Can you think of other things that you could print on? You can find out how we made our block prints on pages 22 and 23.

You will need some thick cardboard to make your printing blocks. Ask a grown-up to cut squares from an old corrugated cardboard box. Look for interesting shapes to stick onto your blocks. Wait until the glue is dry before painting the blocks with thick paint.

We used thin and thick string to make the printing blocks on this page. You can glue the string down to make any shape you like. It is best for making round and swirly patterns. If you want to use two colors, you will have to make two printing blocks – one for each color.

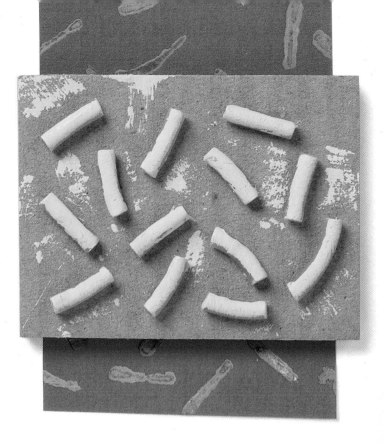

To make a pattern like the one below, ask a grown-up to cut a kitchen sponge into squares. Stick the pieces onto a printing block. Cover the pieces of sponge with thick paint and make a print.

Dry macaroni makes good printing blocks and comes in all shapes and sizes. It is best to use smooth macaroni rather than the kind with ridges. Try sticking dry spaghetti onto a printing block to make a striped pattern.

Try using two different printing blocks side by side to make an interesting pattern. You could also try printing one block on top of another but wait for the first print to dry. Can you think of any other things that would make good printing blocks?

Index

Photographs
By Jon Barnes: 2,3,6,7,8,9,10,11
By Toby: 4,5,12,13,14,15,16,17,18,19,20,21,22,23

Originally published in Great Britain by Two-Can Publishing Ltd.

Library of Congress Card Number: 91-066658

ISBN 0-590-45739-X

All rights reserved, published by Scholastic Inc., 730 Broadway, New York, NY 10003, by arrangement with Two-Can Publishing Ltd.

CARTWHEEL BOOKS is a trademark of Scholastic Inc.

12 11 10 9 8 7 6 5 4 3 2 1   2 3 4 5 6 7/9

Printed in Hong Kong

First Scholastic printing, August 1992